An Introduction to Coping with Panic

2nd Edition

Charles Young

ROBINSON

ROBINSON

First published in Great Britain in 2007 by Robinson,
an imprint of Constable & Robinson Ltd

This edition published in 2017 by Robinson

1 3 5 7 9 10 8 6 4 2

A CIP catalogue record for this book
is available from the British Library.

Important note
This book is not intended as a substitute for medical advice or treatment.
Any person with a condition requiring medical attention should
consult a qualified medical practitioner or suitable therapist.

ISBN: 978-1-47213-853-8

Typeset in Bembo by Initial Typesetting Services, Edinburgh
Printed and bound in Great Britain by CPI Group (UK) Ltd,
Croydon CR0 4YY

Papers used by Robinson are from well-managed forests
and other responsible sources.

Robinson
An imprint of
Little, Brown Book Group
Carmelite House
50 Victoria Embankment
London EC4Y 0DZ

An Hachette UK Company
www.hachette.co.uk

www.littlebrown.co.uk
www.overcoming.co.uk

Contents

About This Book

This book will help you understand and overcome your panic attacks. Part 1 describes what panic attacks are and Part 2 describes what practical steps you can take to overcome them.

It's very important that you read and work through the book from the beginning to the end, As you do so, you may need to return to earlier chapters to ensure that you are very familiar with all the material. Overcoming panic attacks takes hard work and you have to keep at it. The more effort you put into it, the more likely it is that you'll get better, and this will make all the effort worthwhile. But don't feel that you have to get everything right first time. Setbacks are a normal part of getting better and you can learn a lot from them. You'll find throughout this book exercises for you to do. Keep a notebook handy to write down your responses to questions and to make copies of the tables in.

This book is written for you to use on your own. However, if you find that you don't make as much progress as you'd like, you could ask your GP to put you in touch with a cognitive therapist to help you work through the material.

Charles Young

Part 1: ABOUT PANIC

1

Anxiety and Panic

Anxiety, which can range from mild feelings of being nervous, on edge or frightened to sheer terror, is a normal – and essential – part of being human. Although the experience of anxiety is harmless, it's unpleasant for a reason: in order to draw our attention to danger. It is for this adaptive reason that anxiety is not easily ignored.

To understand this better, imagine that you're standing on the edge of a cliff. Most of us would feel a bit anxious staring down a cliff face, particularly if there were no barriers to prevent us from falling over. In fact, our feeling of anxiety would probably make us step back from the edge or, if we decided not to move away, at least take great care. Anxiety is meant to keep us safe.

Anxiety also prepares the body to respond to the danger. This is known as the fight-or-flight response. So, when we get anxious, our bodies get ready to respond quickly and firmly in the face of a physical threat. For instance:

- Our minds become alert and focused on the threat.
- Our heart rate speeds up and blood pressure rises. Meanwhile, blood is sent to the muscles and the muscles tense up in readiness for action.
- We start to sweat more to maintain our body temperature.
- We start to breathe more rapidly, and our nostrils and the air passages in our lungs open wider to allow air in and out more quickly.
- Our livers release sugar to provide quick energy.
- Hormones are released, particularly adrenaline.
- Our blood-clotting ability increases, preparing for possible injury.
- Non-essential processes, such as digestion and saliva production, slow down, causing a dry mouth, 'butterflies in the stomach' and, sometimes, nausea.
- Our sphincter muscles contract (tighten) to close the openings of our bowels and bladder.

This fight-or-flight response is very useful in the short term, helping us to react quickly to immediate physical danger. In the long-distant past humans had to deal with physical dangers all the time, so this response became, and still is, an inbuilt part of our bodily make-up. However, nowadays, many of the dangers we face are non-physical. For instance, we may experience anxiety when we have to speak in public, have relationship problems, or are worried about being able to pay the mortgage. The fight-or-flight response is not at all helpful for dealing with threats like these.

Another problem is that we sometimes see harmless events as dangerous, and this can cause unhelpful anxiety. This is exactly what happens when you experience a panic attack. When you panic, you do so because you regard the symptoms of anxiety as dangerous. For example, a man who fears that he may have a heart attack might think that his racing heart (a normal symptom of anxiety) is the beginning of a heart attack. This thought makes him even more anxious and his heart beats even more rapidly. Like a fire alarm that keeps going off for no good reason, panic attacks are brought on when you see unpleasant yet harmless symptoms of anxiety as signs of a disaster or catastrophe that is about to happen.

Fortunately, it's possible to overcome panic attacks. This book will help you understand exactly what happens when you panic, and teach you to change the thoughts and behaviour that make you have panic attacks. As you become more confident, you'll slowly become able to face the situations that have previously caused you to panic.

2

What Is a Panic Attack?

How do you know if you're having a panic attack? Panic attacks have four characteristics:

1. During panic attacks you experience intense fear or terror.

2. The attack comes on suddenly, often with little warning.

3. The very intense feelings tend to pass quite quickly, often within 5 or 10 minutes. (However, it may not feel quick when it happens, and can leave you feeling very drained and unsettled for a long time afterwards.)

4. During the attack you think that something really awful is about to happen or has already started to happen. You may think you're having a heart attack, or are about to suffocate. Alternatively, you may think you are going to faint, vomit, go crazy, make a fool of yourself, or lose control of your bowels.

Panic attacks are common: As many as one in ten

people will have an occasional panic attack in their lives, and around 3 per cent of all people, perhaps more, will struggle with recurrent panic attacks. Women are more frequently affected than men. Problems with panic attacks are rare amongst children, more common amongst teenagers and most common amongst adults. Despite being common, panic attacks can be very debilitating, preventing people from doing many of the things they enjoyed before their panic attacks started. People who have ongoing problems with panic may need the help of a psychologist, GP or therapist. This can happen because our natural response to panic often makes the situation worse. Fortunately, with help and guidance, people can usually make a lot of progress in overcoming panic attacks. The process of recovery starts with understanding exactly what drives the panic cycle.

How does a panic attack feel?

In the left columns of the three tables on pages 10–15 you will find a list of the common symptoms, thoughts and behaviours associated with panic. Now think about your most recent panic attack and write down the symptoms that apply to you in your notebook or tick the boxes in the table. If you experience any symptoms, thoughts or behaviours that are not listed below, add them to your list.

☐ ☐ ☐ ☐ ☐ ☐ ☐ ☐

Common physical symptoms of panic

- A racing heart
- Feeling faint and dizzy
- Feeling short of breath
- Feeling sick or nauseous
- Feeling that you need to get to a toilet in a hurry
- Experiencing hot flushes
- Experiencing numbness or tingling in your fingertips or toes
- Feeling disconnected from your environment as if you're not really there, or your environment is somehow different or strange

- Sweating, particularly on the palms of your hands, in your armpits and/or on your brow

- Feeling shaky

Any other physical symptoms (list them here)

☐ ☐ ☐ ☐ ☐ ☐ ☐ ☐ ☐

Common Thoughts

- I'm going to have a heart attack

- I'm about to collapse or faint

- I'm suffocating/struggling to breathe

- I'm about to lose control of my bladder or bowels

- I'm going to choke to death

- I'm going 'mad'

- I'm about to vomit

- I'm about to lose control and do something crazy

- I'm making a complete fool of myself in front of others

Any other frightening thoughts (list them here)

Common Behaviours

☐ ☐

- An overwhelming need to escape the situation and return to a place of safety

- A desire to avoid the places or situations where I've had panic attacks

Any actions taken to escape or avoid either of the behaviours that you ticked above (list them here)

3

The Panic Vicious Circle

Once you've had one panic attack, you're often frightened of having another one, and become very sensitive to the normal symptoms of anxiety that we all have from time to time. People often worry that these are signs of another panic attack. This worry results in greater anxiety, which may in turn bring about another panic attack.

Take the example of Emily, a 25-year-old woman and marketing assistant at the head office of a large UK retailer. A year ago she vomited on a stuffy, crowded train between Cambridge and London the morning after eating a dodgy meal at a late-night restaurant with friends. She felt very embarrassed and ashamed and fled the train at the next stop. After this, she noticed that she became very anxious in public places. Recently, at a busy work seminar, where she had to present sales figures to the senior management, she began to feel anxious and nauseous. She was afraid that she would vomit in front of all her colleagues and quickly had to leave the room. Emily was in a state of terror. She was sweating, she felt dizzy, her heart was pounding and she was taking short, rapid breaths. She went to a bathroom and splashed some water on her face, while making sure that she took deep breaths. She recovered after around 10 minutes, but felt very drained for the rest of the day. She is convinced that if she had not left the moment she did, she would have vomited and this would've been very damaging to her career. This type of thing is happening to Emily more and more often.

Emily's panic attacks

Emily's panic attacks seem to be triggered by anything that causes her to become a bit anxious. In particular, she becomes anxious in social situations where she can't easily escape to a bathroom. Other triggers include normal feelings in her stomach that most of us would hardly notice.

As soon as she notices that she's starting to feel uncomfortable, she thinks: 'What if I throw up?' This makes her much more anxious. She begins to sweat more than usual, her heart beats much more quickly, she feels slightly nauseous and has a dry mouth. She also notices that she gets shaky and can't keep her mind on anything other than her anxiety. Emily feels short of breath and begins to breathe more rapidly, which always makes her feel worse.

As Emily experiences these symptoms, which she associates with being sick, she feels sure that she'll vomit. As soon as she believes that she's about to vomit, she becomes more anxious and her symptoms of anxiety get worse, and so on.

Emily has never vomited since the time when she was on the train, and afterwards her GP diagnosed a mild case of food poisoning. However, since then, she has avoided trains and restaurants.

From the sequence of events that occurred when Emily had her recent panic attack, it is clear that panic is a rapid of escalation of anxiety that can be described as a vicious circle. Generally, the sequence of panic is as follows: An event triggers initial anxiety. The person notices the mental sensations or symptoms that are a harmless part of anxiety, and misinterprets these as a sign of some sort of impending catastrophe. This catastrophic misinterpretation causes more anxiety and the cycle goes on. See the diagram opposite.

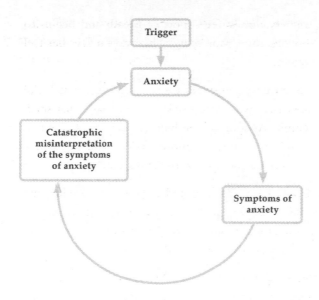

Emily's vicious circle

This idea of a vicious circle becomes clearer when we look again at what happened when Emily had her recent panic attack. She was at her work seminar and had the thought, 'what if I throw up in front of my colleagues?' This made her feel very uneasy and perhaps it was then that she first noticed a slight twinge in her stomach. She then interpreted this and other symptoms of her anxiety, especially the mild nausea and bodily discomfort, as a sign that she was about to vomit, which made her much more anxious and which made her symptoms of anxiety worse. And so it went until she fled the scene and slowly recovered. The anxiety associated with the thought that she might vomit in front of her colleagues was exacerbated because she believed that this would have had serious negative implications for her career. See the diagram below.

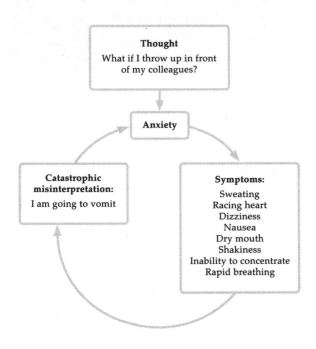

Your vicious circle

Now it is your turn. You can copy the diagram below to map out your own most recent or vivid panic attack. The checklists on pages 10–15 will help you complete the diagram and see exactly why and how the panic attack occurred. Ask yourself, 'What symptoms of anxiety did I notice when I became anxious? What did I think was the worst thing that was happening to me when I noticed these symptoms (even though I now know that this did not happen)?'

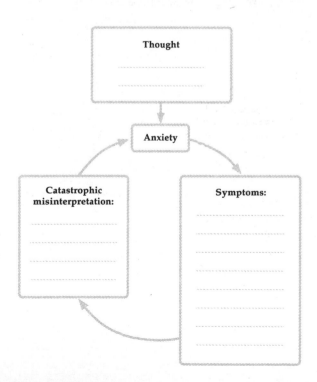

Does this make sense to you? Can you see how your thinking may have made the experience of anxiety worse, resulting in panic?

4

Thoughts and Panic

When you think that harmless, though uncomfortable, symptoms of anxiety are signs of a much
more serious problem, you become more anxious.
And when you think these symptoms are signs of
a catastrophe that is about to happen, you panic.
Usually, there's a logical connection between the
main anxiety symptoms you have and the catastrophic misinterpretations made. In the table over-
leaf, the left-hand column lists common symptoms
of anxiety, and the right-hand column lists the
ways in which people commonly misjudge these
symptoms.

It's very important to realise that it is the catastrophic
misinterpretation that drives the vicious circle. If
you can remind yourself that these uncomfortable
symptoms of anxiety are harmless, there's nothing
to drive the cycle and the anxiety doesn't grow into
panic. The question, then, is: how do we challenge
these misinterpretations? A good place to start is to
consider some facts about these common fears.

Main anxiety symptoms	Likely catastrophic misinterpretations
Pounding heart, palpitations and chest pain	I'm having a heart attack
Shortness of breath	I'm going to suffocate
Feeling dizzy, unsteady or having 'jelly legs'	I'm about to collapse or faint
Pins and needles or numbness	I'm having a stroke
Racing thoughts	I'm losing my mind
Blurred vision	I'm going blind
Feeling of unreality, lack of concentration or unusual mental sensations	I'm going mad or I am going to have a stroke
Sudden urge to go to the toilet	I'm going to lose control of my bowels or bladder

Fear of having a heart attack or stroke

Some of the symptoms of panic, particularly chest pain, are similar to those that people expect to experience during a heart attack. It's therefore understandable that if you're having a panic attack, you may think that you are in fact having a heart attack. However, it's worth remembering that heart disease is very rare in young women, who also happen to be the group most likely to experience panic attacks. If you do have repeated chest pain, then you should go and see your doctor as soon as possible. However, if your doctor has already ruled out any heart problems then it's very unlikely that your chest pain is caused by problems with your heart. The pain and rapid or unusual heartbeat are most likely caused by the anxiety. If you've had panic attacks that made you think you have a heart problem, then ask yourself: 'Did I have a heart attack the last time I felt this way?' If not, why should it be any different this time? In the same way, if your fear is about having a stroke, then ask yourself: 'If it didn't happen last time, why would it happen this time?'

Fear of going crazy

When you're having a panic attack you may think you're starting to lose touch with reality and are going insane. This thought will naturally make you anxious and so the cycle goes on. If this is one of your concerns, remember there's a big difference between panic and severe mental illness. Panic attacks and other anxiety problems are a very common part of normal human experience, while severe mental illnesses (such as schizophrenia or bipolar disorder) are rare. Panic attacks do not cause mental illness. And if you have panic attacks you're no more likely than anyone else to develop a severe mental illness.

You may feel very disconnected from your surroundings when you get panicky. Things and places seem somehow different, or you feel strange or unusual. Often, people assume that these feelings are signs of a severe mental illness. But in fact they are just another common, normal and completely harmless symptom of anxiety.

Fear of fainting

People faint because their blood pressure is too low and not enough oxygen is getting to the brain. The most obvious result of fainting is that you fall over. Once you're lying down, your heart is at the same level as your brain and no longer has to pump blood 'uphill'. Also, your muscles relax, releasing blood that can then flow into your brain. As a result, your blood pressure quickly rises and you soon recover. Like anxiety, fainting is another way your body protects you from harm.

Now, think about what happens during a panic attack. As soon as you become anxious, your heart beats much faster than usual and your blood pressure rises. This is exactly the opposite of what happens when you faint. Although you may be afraid you'll faint while panicking, this doesn't happen.

You may have heard of people who faint at the sight of blood or injury (or even needles). This is known as a *blood–injury phobia* and is different from what happens when people have a panic attack. People with this type of phobia react differently from others when they are faced with their fear. Instead of rising, their blood pressure drops. People who have this type of phobia can be taught a specific technique called *applied tension* that increases blood pressure. However, unless you have this rare problem (and you would know if you did), it's best just to remind yourself that you are actually less likely to faint while panicking than you are at any other time.

Fear of losing control

Your greatest fear may be that when you become very anxious you'll lose control and you'll run around wildly, hurting yourself or others, while screaming and shouting nonsense. In fact, there has never been a documented case of anybody doing anything 'out of control' in this way while having a panic attack. If you're worried about losing control when panicking ask yourself: 'Did I do something completely out of control the last time I had a panic attack?' If not, why should it be any different this time?

Fear of suffocating

One of the most common symptoms of anxiety is rapid breathing, which causes some people to fear they are suffocating. Rapid breathing is a normal part of the 'fight-or-flight response' (see pages 5–7), enabling your muscles to get more oxygen in order to prepare to fight or to run away from danger. However, breathing too quickly, while not harmful, can increase many panic symptoms, such as feeling faint, tingling sensations, dizziness and being out of breath. Indeed, for many people, the worst symptoms of panic happen as a result of their breathing. This is because rapid breathing changes the oxygen and carbon dioxide levels in our blood. We breathe in oxygen and breathe out carbon dioxide. The balance is upset when we breathe more quickly than our bodies need us to, and we end up with too much oxygen in the bloodstream. This is called hyperventilation.

When the delicate balance between oxygen and carbon dioxide is upset, we tend to feel out of breath and so breathe even faster, though what we need is less oxygen rather than more. For this reason, breathing into a paper bag when you're hyperventilating can be helpful, because you re-breathe the carbon dioxide that you have breathed out. This increases the level of carbon dioxide in your blood, correcting the balance. However, a better way to restore this balance is to breathe in a controlled way, which will be explained in chapter 6 (see pages 47–9).

If you're someone who worries about suffocating, you may find that you avoid small, enclosed spaces because you fear that there won't be enough oxygen for you to breathe. This fear may trigger a panic attack. But even small rooms have tens of thousands of litres of air for us to breathe, which is more air than anybody would need to survive for many hours even if the room was sealed shut. However, the rooms we use in everyday life are not airtight. You can test this by asking a friend to spray some air freshener around the edge of a closed door. If the smell of the freshener leaks through, you can be sure that the air supply flows in and out through the smallest gaps more quickly than we need it.

Others fear that they won't be able to breathe when it's too hot. However, warm air is just as rich in oxygen as cold air. Opening windows or using a fan may make us feel better, but this isn't necessary for us to be able to breathe.

Fear of losing control of bowels or bladder

Another common fear is that you'll lose control of your bowels or bladder while panicking – but in fact this doesn't seem to happen, unless you've had a very bad stomach bug. You may have the urge to use a toilet, but this is not the same as losing control of your bladder or bowels. Indeed, one of the symptoms of becoming anxious is that the sphincter muscles tighten or contract. For instance, some people suffer from a common phobia known as 'paruresis'; the struggle to urinate in the presence of others. The question to ask yourself, again, is: 'If it didn't happen last time, why should it happen this time?'

Fear of vomiting

In a similar way you may be afraid of vomiting while panicking, just like Emily in the example above – yet very few people ever claim to have actually vomited during a panic attack. You may feel nauseous when you get anxious, but that does not mean that you will be sick. Think about how often you have felt nauseous without vomiting.

These are only a few examples of the common mis-interpretations that we make when we panic. The second part of this book will help you challenge these and any other thoughts that turn normal anxiety into panic.

Part 2: COPING WITH PANIC

5

The Panic Diary

A panic diary is an excellent way of collecting important facts to help you challenge the thoughts that turn ordinary anxiety into a panic attack. After every panic attack, you should use the diary to record the date, situation, main symptoms of anxiety, catastrophic misinterpretation of the anxiety and, once you have had some practice, a response to the catastrophic misinterpretation. Let's take Emily's most recent panic attack at her work seminar as an example, and record the details in the first four columns of the diary as follows (leaving out the alternative response for the moment):

PANIC DIARY

Date	Situation	Anxiety symptoms	Catastrophic misinterpretation	Alternative response
25 Feb	At work, attending a crowded seminar	Sweaty Racing heart Dizzy Nausea Dry mouth Shaky Unable to concentrate Rapid breathing	I'm going to throw up in front of all my colleagues and ruin my career	

The final column is where Emily would think of a helpful response to her catastrophic misinterpretation that she was about to *throw up in front of her work colleagues and ruin her career*. What could you say to her to weaken her belief that she's about to vomit? Write down your answer.

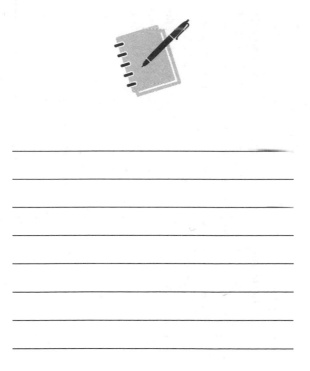

Now it is your turn to think about your most recent or most vivid panic attack. Use the diary below or copy the columns and headings of the panic diary into your notebook. Think back to what you were doing right before the panic attack and remember all that happened afterwards until the panic attack had passed.

To start with, focus on the first four columns and leave the alternative response for the time being. Record the date (and the time if you have more than one panic attack in a day), and then make a brief note of the situation, describing where you were and what you were doing, in the second column. Then list your symptoms in the third column, using the list of common symptoms on pages 10–11 if you need to. Now write down the most frightening thoughts that went through your mind before or during the panic attack in the fourth column. If you struggle to identify the catastrophic misinterpretation, ask yourself what was the worst thing that you thought could happen to you while you were panicking.

PANIC DIARY

Date	Situation	Anxiety symptoms	Catastrophic misinterpretation	Alternative response

Finding an alternative response to the catastrophic thought

Once you have completed the first four columns of the panic diary, you can start to challenge the catastrophic misinterpretation by asking yourself: 'I've had many previous panic attacks, so why has my worst fear not already occurred?' On a new page, write down your answer in your notebook.

_____

_____

_____

_____

_____

_____

_____

Now ask yourself: 'Is there any reason to think that it'll be any different this time?' Write down your answer in your notebook.

_____

_____

_____

_____

_____

_____

_____

Another way to challenge your own catastrophic thoughts is to ask yourself: 'What would a close friend say to comfort me while I was having a panic attack?' Write down what you think they'd say. Or: 'What would I say to a friend who described a panic attack to me?' Write down your thoughts.

_____

_____

_____

_____

_____

_____

_____

_____

If you know that what you have is just anxiety, but still fear the catastrophic misinterpretation, then you may want to ask yourself: 'How does anxiety cause the terrifying event that I think is going to happen when I panic? For example, how does being anxious cause me to vomit, have a heart attack, faint, etc.?' What's a less extreme way of looking at this situation? Make a note of your thoughts.

_____

_____

_____

_____

_____

_____

Having asked all or some of these questions of your catastrophic misinterpretations, choose your best answer or come up with a short response based on a number of your answers and copy this into the last column of the panic diary.

From now on, record the date, situation, anxiety symptoms, catastrophic misinterpretation and alternative response each time you experience a panic attack. With practice, you will find out which of the questions listed above work best for you, or you might even come up with your own questions. The important thing is to keep at it by questioning the catastrophic misinterpretations until they lose their power to make you anxious. Continue to practise this for as long as it takes to replace what has usually become a habitual way of anxious thinking with a new habitual, more helpful way of thinking. For many people, this takes weeks if not months.

6

Correcting Your Breathing

What happens when you hyperventilate?

Hyperventilation plays an important role in most panic attacks; so let's see how it works. Sit down in a comfortable chair and imagine that you are blowing up a large inflatable mattress. Breathe in and out quickly, making sure that you blow hard to fill the mattress. To start with, try to do this for 10 seconds, then 15 seconds, and so on, until you can hyperventilate for 30 to 45 seconds. This will make you feel very uncomfortable. If you aren't able or willing to do this on your own, ask a friend or healthcare professional to help you. In your notebook list the sensations you feel when you breathe much more rapidly than usual.

Could some of the symptoms that you have experienced during a panic attack be caused by the way you breathe? If so, which ones? Write them down in your notebook.

Small changes to how quickly you breathe can upset the delicate balance between oxygen and carbon dioxide in the bloodstream. This can cause unpleasant symptoms, including:

1. Tingling face, hands or limbs

2. Muscle tremors or cramps

3. Dizziness and visual problems

4. Difficulty breathing

5. Exhaustion and feelings of fatigue

6. Chest and stomach discomfort

You can easily correct over-breathing by learning to breathe gently and evenly. Controlled breathing can help you prevent the uncomfortable symptoms of hyperventilating to manage your anxiety better. While it may not be the answer for everyone, you'll only know if it works for you if you practise it for 2 or 3 minutes as often as you can (and at least 3 or 4 times a day). The better you are at controlling your breathing when you are relaxed, the better you will be at controlling your breathing when you are anxious.

Controlled breathing

Either sit upright or lie down on your back. If possible, breathe through your nose in a gentle, steady rhythm. Your breathing should not be jerky and you should try not to gulp or gasp.

1. Place one hand on your chest and one hand on your stomach.

2. As you breathe in through your nose, allow your stomach to swell. This means that you're using your lungs fully. Try to keep the movement in your upper chest to a minimum and keep the movement gentle. Imagine that you have four lungs: two in your chest and two in your stomach area. Imagine the 'lungs' in your stomach filling up with air.

3. Slowly and evenly, breathe out through your nose. Now imagine the 'lungs' in your stomach area deflating.

4. Repeat this to establish a gentle rhythm. You're aiming to take 8 to 12 breaths a minute. This means that it should take around 5 to 7 seconds for each in-breath and out-breath cycle. But don't worry too much about the timing – you'll find a comfortable rhythm that's right for you.

5. Try to relax your mind too. Shut your eyes and concentrate on pleasant, peaceful thoughts. Feel the tensions ease in your body.

Remember to practise this exercise often. The more you practise, the more easily you will realise when you aren't breathing correctly and be able to adjust this when necessary.

7

Challenging Safety and Avoidance Behaviours

It's normal to try to protect yourself when you feel that something bad may happen. Safety behaviours are the things you **do** to prevent the catastrophe that you think is going to happen to you when you panic. Avoidance behaviours are the things that you **don't do** in order to prevent the catastrophe.

Imagine a man who believes that he'll faint while he's having one of his frequent panic attacks. He struggles to do his shopping because he is frightened that he might faint in the supermarket. So he'll only go to the supermarket after a few pints of beer because alcohol makes him less anxious. This is a safety behaviour (which could be rather unsafe!). If he refuses to go to the supermarket at all, this is an avoidance behaviour. Most of us use both, though we are often more aware of the avoidance behaviours than we are of the safety ones.

Sometimes the avoidance is extreme and people are unable to leave what they consider their 'safety zones', usually their homes. Other people have a very fixed routine that takes them from home to work and back again, and they get very anxious if this routine is broken or changed in any way. These are examples of agoraphobia, a condition that sometimes occurs as a result of panic attacks. However, not everybody who has panic attacks is agoraphobic.

With panic attacks, because the danger isn't real, these safety and avoidance behaviours only make things worse. They prevent you from realising that what you're dreading isn't going to happen. Also, your brain responds to what you do. So if you tell yourself that there's no real danger, but continue to behave as if there is a danger, your brain will make you feel anxious. You have to show your brain that the danger isn't real by behaving as if the danger were not real.

Some safety behaviours can cause the very sensations that are then catastrophically misinterpreted. Take the example of the man who fears fainting in public and who must drink a few pints of beer before visiting the supermarket. One too many beers and he feels a little dizzy and faint.

By using safety and avoidance behaviours, you're telling yourself that you can't really cope in anxiety-provoking situations without them. This makes you feel less confident and is likely to make you more anxious.

Jim's avoidance behaviour

Jim, a 48-year-old builder, has a history of panic attacks. During his attacks, he often believes that he is having a heart attack. He interprets his symptoms – usually a pounding heart, shortness of breath and faintness – as proof that there's something very wrong with his heart. Frightened that he may die of a heart attack, Jim avoids energetic activity. Because of this, he's less fit than he used to be and finds himself out of breath after even a short walk. This in turn convinces him that there must be something wrong with his heart. His avoidance behaviour has directly increased his anxiety symptoms.

Jim's safety behaviour

Jim takes an aspirin every day, even though his doctor has told him that because he does not have a cardiovascular disease, there is no need for him to do so – and that for him, the risk of side effects from using aspirin every day outweighs the benefits. The act of taking his pills only reinforces his fear that he is at very high risk of having a heart attack.

The diagram below shows a typical panic cycle, illustrating how safety and avoidance behaviours help to keep panic attacks going.

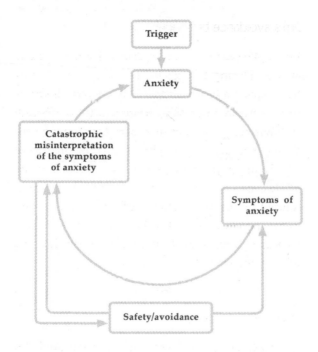

Giving up safety and avoidance behaviours

So, to overcome panic attacks, you need to face up to the situations that you usually avoid. You need to do this without the safety behaviours you normally use. Learning to give up these safety and avoidance behaviours is probably the most important step in overcoming panic, but also one of the most difficult. So take it slowly. To start, have a look at the following list of common safety behaviours.

Common safety behaviours

Here are some examples of common safety behaviours:

- Only going to places with someone else with whom you feel safe.
- Carrying anti-anxiety medication just in case you get anxious, even when you don't often use it.
- Frequently resting in order to 'prevent' a possible heart attack.
- Carrying a plastic bag with you in case you're sick.
- Carrying a paper bag in case you hyperventilate.
- Drinking alcohol before going to places or doing things that make you anxious.
- Sucking a mint or chewing gum in situations that make you anxious.
- Only sitting in an aisle seat at the cinema.
- Taking a fully-charged mobile phone wherever you go so that you can call for help.

• Taking spare clothes and underwear with you wherever you go in case you lose control of your bladder or bowels.

In your notebook make a list of your own safety behaviours.

_____

_____

_____

_____

_____

_____

_____

Now, make a list of the places or things that you deliberately avoid. Also include places or things that you'd *like* to avoid in an ideal world in order not to have a panic attack, but actually have to come into contact with because they are simply unavoidable. Common examples include refusing to go to particular places, such as busy supermarkets, crowded restaurants or cinemas. The task now is to gradually face these situations without your typical safety behaviours. A step-by-step approach to these challenges works best.

Graded exposure

The way to confront situations that you usually try to avoid is to start with the ones that make you the least anxious and work up to the ones that make you the most anxious. This is known as graded exposure.

Stopping safety behaviours and facing up to situations that you fear will probably make you feel anxious. However, you do need to experience the anxiety without the help of your safety behaviours in order to get rid of any remaining belief that the scenario you fear may actually happen.

Also, the longer you're able to stay in the situation, the less anxious you'll eventually start to feel, because you are showing your brain that it needn't make you anxious. This is known as desensitisation.

You will need to rate the intensity of your feelings of anxiety using a scale of 0 to 100, where 100 means the worst anxiety that you have ever experienced, while 0 means a state where you are completely calm. Look at how Emily ranked the situations that she'd usually avoid:

Rank 0–100	Situation	Anxiety rating 0–100
1	Presenting a seminar to boss and clients	95
2	Taking a train to London	90
3	Attending weekly business meetings	85
4	Shopping at the supermarket	55
5	Going out for dinner	45

Using the table below, and with the help of your list of situations that you avoid or must endure only in very specific situations with safety behaviours (see page 55), rate each one according to how anxious you think you would be if you were in that situation.

Rank 0–100	Situation	Anxiety rating 0–100
1		
2		
3		
4		
5		

You may need to spend some time adjusting your list as you think more about the situations that make you anxious and break down some of the difficult ones into easier steps. For example, Emily recalled that shopping at the supermarket was worse on a Saturday when it was very busy, while it was much easier during the week. The important thing is to make progress, however slowly, taking on each challenge step by step. For Emily, this meant starting her exposure work at the supermarket when it was least busy and then when it was busier before confronting the supermarket on a very busy Saturday afternoon at the end of the month. So, for example, if supermarkets frighten you, you could start with your local shop, and then move on to a slightly bigger store, before visiting a supermarket.

Before you start to actually face these situations, there are some techniques you should employ to help you manage your anxiety in the situations, while also tracking and recording your anxiety at the start and end of the exposure.

Helpful techniques: coping statements and controlled breathing

When you do face up to situations that make you anxious, it's helpful to think of a coping statement that you can repeat to yourself as you get panicky. For example, many people find it helpful to tell themselves:

'This is just a panic attack. It'll pass and I'll feel better. When it does pass, I'll feel much more confident about dealing with these situations in the future.'

Make a note of a coping statement that you think will be useful for you.

_____

_____

_____

_____

_____

_____

_____

Also, remember to control your breathing when you confront situations that you've avoided up until now. Controlled breathing (see pages 47–8) prevents the symptoms of anxiety from becoming more severe. Breathing slowly will also help to calm you down and distract you from the catastrophic thoughts you have when you panic.

As you become more confident that panic attacks are harmless, it'll become easier to drop your safety behaviours and face the situations that you've been avoiding.

Recording your graded exposure

Now that your list of avoided situations is complete and you are ready to face these situations, you should copy them into the table below, in order from least to most anxiety, with a rating of how anxious you expect each one to make you feel in the second column.

In turn, confront each situation, preferably without any safety behaviours, and record how anxious you are at first. Is the actual anxiety as bad as you expected? Stay in the situation, if you can, until your anxiety has come down to, at most, 20 or 30 on your scale.

Situation	Expected anxiety 0–100	Anxiety rating at the start 0–100	Anxiety rating at the end 0–100

Keep confronting the situations until they no longer cause you such anxiety. See this as an important series of steps not only to overcome your panic attacks but also to reclaim aspects of your life that were taken by your panic attacks. Reward yourself for your successes. Draw inspiration to continue to face your fears from the two examples that are based on real cases in the next chapter.

8

Two Case Studies

You may find it helpful to read about others who have put many of these strategies into practice in order to overcome their panic attacks.

Lynn's story

Lynn's first panic attacks

Lynn was a 29-year-old nursing assistant who had a severe panic attack while visiting a seaside town with friends on her day off. She was browsing in a shop when she started to feel that she was having difficulty breathing. This may have had something to do with the effort of walking around on an extremely hot day. She also felt as if she couldn't swallow. Understandably, Lynn became extremely anxious. She felt faint and thought that she'd collapse. At the time Lynn believed that she was going into shock. She had to lie down on the floor of the shop while her friends called an ambulance. Lynn was raced to hospital and while in the ambulance she was convinced that she was about to die.

However, when she arrived at the hospital the doctors could find nothing wrong with her. She was kept under observation for a few hours and then sent home without any explanation for what had happened to her. The doctors at the hospital gave her a packet of tranquillisers and told her to use the medication every day, but she decided against this.

Lynn had a few more panic attacks in the following weeks. Although she felt like calling an ambulance, she was able to stop herself. She did call a helpline and the healthcare worker who answered suggested that she was having a panic attack. Lynn doubted that this could explain her symptoms, which were so bad. A few weeks later Lynn's GP referred her to a psychologist with a note saying that he thought Lynn had had some sort of traumatic reaction to the terrifying experience of being rushed to the accident and emergency department.

Identifying the vicious circle of panic

At her first meeting with the psychologist, Lynn described everything that had happened. It was clear that Lynn had experienced a severe panic attack while out with her friends and that since then she'd had a series of less severe panic attacks.

The psychologist explained the vicious circle of panic. Although Lynn still had her doubts, she could see that her catastrophic misinterpretation that she was about to die could have made her physical symptoms worse. The psychologist gave Lynn a booklet to take away and read before the next appointment.

Lynn found the booklet very reassuring. At her next meeting with the psychologist she explained that she would never have believed that a panic attack could be so frightening. At this meeting, Lynn's psychologist introduced the panic diary and asked Lynn to complete it each time she had an attack.

Using a panic diary

Lynn returned a week later. She'd used her diary to record a panic attack that had happened a few days earlier. One night, when her housemate was away, Lynn became increasingly anxious as she got ready for bed. As she went up the stairs, she felt out of breath and started to worry that she'd collapse and nobody would be around to help her. She became very agitated and began to breathe rapidly. As she did this, she started to feel more and more out of breath. However, she was able to tell herself that this was only a panic attack and that it would soon pass. In time it did and Lynn was eventually able to get to sleep. She put the phone next to her bed in case she needed to call an ambulance during the night.

When Lynn later filled in the diary she could see that what she'd experienced was nothing more than a panic attack.

Learning controlled breathing

At the next meeting with her psychologist, Lynn agreed to try a hyperventilation exercise. During the meeting, she made herself breathe rapidly and quickly felt all the symptoms that she normally experienced while panicking, so that she had to stop. Her psychologist encouraged her to try again. Lynn did, but was sure that she would pass out. She was amazed to see how much her breathing had to do with her experience of panic. She was able to hyperventilate for more than 30 seconds and when she was sure she would pass out, her psychologist asked her to stand up. She did this and was surprised to find that she didn't collapse. She realised that the problem wasn't that she would pass out but rather that she *thought* that she would pass out.

Later on in the session, the psychologist taught Lynn how to control her breathing. She practised this 4 or 5 times every day.

Whenever she felt very anxious, Lynn was able to control her breathing and she started to realise that she could cope with the panic attacks.

In her panic diary, she was soon responding to her catastrophic thoughts by telling herself that the fact that she had not died meant that all she was having was a panic attack and this would do her no harm.

Confronting safety and avoidance behaviours

Lynn's panic attacks started to happen less often and she noticed that they weren't nearly as bad as her first ones. She spoke to her psychologist about her safety behaviours and the things that she'd been avoiding. For example, Lynn had made sure that she was never too far from a hospital just in case she needed emergency medical treatment. She used to enjoy walking in the country, but she'd given this up, fearing that if she had an attack when no one was around to help her she might die.

Lynn also used a number of safety behaviours. She wouldn't go anywhere without her mobile phone, and always made sure that it was charged and topped up in case she had to dial 999. She carried a paper bag with her wherever she went, in case she hyperventilated. She also carried the packet of tranquillisers the hospital doctors had given her, even though she had decided against using them.

However, as Lynn progressed with her therapy, she was slowly able to go further and further away from her home (which was very close to the hospital where she worked). She went out a few times without her mobile phone and threw away the paper bag. Although she was more anxious, Lynn was delighted to find that she could go for long walks again. In time, she stopped worrying about her phone. She was able to go with her friends on a hike in the Peak District, where she knew that she would not easily be able to get to a hospital. By this time, Lynn was confident that she'd cope and she noticed that she hadn't had a panic attack for weeks.

A few months later, Lynn went on a charity hike in South Africa. Before seeing her psychologist, she was sure that she would have to withdraw, even though she'd been looking forward to it for more than a year. Lynn was worried that she wouldn't get adequate medical help if she needed it. However, she decided that she needed to do the trip to prove to herself that she had really put the panic attacks behind her.

Success

Not surprisingly, Lynn had a wonderful time and returned full of confidence. She explained to her psychologist in their final meeting that her family and friends had told her that she was back to normal. Lynn and her psychologist were delighted with her progress.

Jason's story

An alarming experience

Jason was a 27-year-old manager of a mobile phone store. He used cannabis one evening with his friends and became very paranoid, convinced that he was going crazy and about to lose control of himself. Jason begged his friends to take him to a psychiatric hospital, but they were unsympathetic and found the whole episode very funny. He eventually went to sleep; the next day he felt slightly traumatised, but otherwise OK, and vowed never to use the drug again.

Fear of losing control

However, the fear of losing control didn't go away, and Jason had a panic attack a few days later while shopping in the high street on a busy Saturday afternoon. He started to feel very strange – as if everywhere around him was different and he was strangely unreal. His heart was pounding and his mind was full of racing thoughts. He felt unable to tolerate all of the noise and movement around him. Jason imagined that he was about to lose control and run around with his arms flapping, shouting nonsense, and perhaps even attacking strangers in the street. He pictured men in white coats strapping him to a stretcher and taking him away. He imagined his parents' shock as somebody explained that he had been locked away in a psychiatric ward. Jason was terrified and as quickly as he could rushed back to his car to get out of town. The terror passed quite quickly, but Jason believed that this must be an early sign of madness. After this he avoided going into town as much as possible.

Jason had similar panic attacks in the following weeks. Then, one day, while driving on the motorway, he thought: 'What if I drive my car into that oncoming lorry?' This thought seemed to just pop into his head from nowhere, and Jason took it as a further sign that he was going crazy. Thinking that he would lose control of his car, he had to pull over and ask his father to come and fetch him. From that point on he avoided driving faster than 50 miles per hour and driving on motorways; this started to cause problems at work, because Jason needed to attend weekly meetings with his regional manager some distance away.

At the home he shared with his fiancée, Jason made sure that he removed his hammer and other tools from the house, and refused to handle knives just in case he 'did something dreadful'.

He was terrified that he would lose control and hurt his fiancée, or anybody else who happened to be around. He gave up drinking alcohol because he believed that if he lost his inhibitions he'd definitely 'tip over the edge'.

Seeking expert help

Jason's father suggested that he speak to the family GP, but he was terrified of doing this because he thought that his doctor would be obliged to have him admitted to a psychiatric hospital or tell the police that he was a danger to society. However, after another panic attack that forced him to leave work in the middle of the day, Jason and his father did go to see their doctor.

This meeting was a huge relief for Jason. His doctor told him that he was not going crazy but was having panic attacks, and agreed to refer Jason to a psychologist. He decided not to prescribe any medication because Jason explained that, after his experience with cannabis, he did not want to use any psychiatric medication if he could help it.

However, while waiting for the psychology appointment, the reassurance that Jason got from his doctor seemed to disappear and he started to wonder if his doctor had made a mistake. As time passed he became increasingly anxious and, once again, was sure that he was going crazy.

Recognising intrusive thoughts

When Jason met his psychologist a few weeks later, he described everything that had happened.

He also admitted that he'd had strange thoughts about harming people or doing 'crazy things' for many years, but he'd mostly been able to dismiss these. Jason was sure that the psychologist would think he had a serious and dangerous mental illness. However, the psychologist explained that Jason's strange thoughts were in fact just common intrusive thoughts that he didn't need to worry about.

Together, Jason and his psychologist identified the different factors that were driving his panic cycle. Jason's fear that he was going crazy made him more anxious, and the symptoms of this anxiety seemed to confirm the fear that he was going crazy. At the psychologist's suggestion, they went for a drive together in Jason's car. As they drove on to the motorway, Jason became extremely anxious and started to think that he'd lose control. However, his psychologist encouraged him to drive normally and not to slow right down. To his surprise and despite the anxiety, Jason didn't lose control or deliberately crash the vehicle. He gradually started to think that maybe feeling anxious didn't necessarily mean he'd lose control.

As a homework exercise, Jason's psychologist asked him to drive on the motorway on his own every day.

The psychologist had also suggested that Jason complete a panic diary, and, after noting down what happened every time he felt panicky, Jason saw that he only ever thought he was going crazy when he was very anxious. He learned that feeling unreal or strange was a common anxiety symptom. While all these things made him feel much better, Jason still worried that, even if he wasn't mentally ill now, his anxiety could eventually cause him to 'go crazy' sometime in the future. Fortunately, he was able to challenge this incorrect belief that anxiety causes serious mental illness.

A breakthrough

When he next saw his psychologist, Jason was asked to read a series of words such as 'schizophrenia', 'mental illness', 'crazy', 'insane', 'mad' and 'barmy'. While reading these words aloud, Jason started to think that he'd lose control in the psychologist's office and began to feel very anxious. Yet once again, despite feeling very panicky, he didn't lose control, even when encouraged to do so by his psychologist. He now accepted that his problem was that he became anxious whenever he thought that he could go crazy, which made him think that he'd lose control. For the first time, Jason really believed that he was having panic attacks and could see how the cycle of panic was affecting him. With this breakthrough, and because anxiety is far less frightening than going crazy, he noticed that when he got anxious he didn't panic as he had before.

After this session, he decided to tackle a number of situations that he'd been avoiding. He drove on the motorway and across bridges (he'd also feared that he might deliberately drive his car off a bridge), went back to town when it was busy and even had a few drinks. Jason handled knives in the presence of his fiancée and brought the hammer back into the house. Being so pleased with his progress, he wanted to take things further: he began an exercise programme to get fit and decided to give up smoking. Within a few months he felt better than ever – the panic was a thing of the past and he noticed that although he could feel anxious from time to time, he no longer thought that he was going crazy.

9

Continuing Your Recovery

By now, you'll have learned the main practical strategies for overcoming panic attacks. Complete recovery takes a lot of work, and may take some time. Unfortunately, there's no 'quick fix' for panic attacks. You may have to practise the techniques repeatedly to get the hang of them. You'll feel better as you become more confident that panic attacks are harmless. With this growing confidence, you'll notice that your panic attacks occur less frequently and are less intense. You should feel increasingly confident about approaching situations that you've previously avoided. Slowly, you should start to reclaim your life.

Setbacks, however, are a normal part of recovery. In fact, they're often an important part of the process of getting better. So don't be disillusioned if you experience a setback. Simply look back at the earlier sections in this book to understand exactly what has happened. Then use the strategies you've learned to turn the disappointment into a useful experience that will help you make more progress.

Medication

Your GP may have prescribed medication to treat your panic attacks. Various types of medication work in different ways. Some anti-depressant/ anti-anxiety medications and minor tranquillisers are used to make you feel less anxious, while beta-blockers reduce the physical symptoms of anxiety. Some medications only need to be taken when you feel anxious, while others need to be taken at around the same time each day. Occasionally these medicines have side effects, but these usually pass in time. If you have any problems with your medication, then you should discuss these with your GP as soon as possible.

If, after completing this self-help programme, you still suspect that your ability to cope is due to the medication and not because you've overcome your panic attacks, then you should discuss this with your GP, who will advise you accordingly. Medication can become a type of safety behaviour that prevents you from realising that you're able to cope without any special help. However, you shouldn't make any changes involving your medication without talking to your doctor first.

Physical exercise

Exercise is a very useful way of dealing with anxiety; it helps improve anxious and sad moods, can make you feel better about yourself, and a recent study suggests that it can reduce the symptoms of panic. Researchers have found that even a single bout of exercise can have benefits for people who experience panic attacks. If it has been a long time since you last exercised, it is preferable that you speak to your GP or nurse before attempting any serious exercise. Also remember that you might not be able to do as much as you once could, at least at first; you'll probably have to ease yourself back into it. Your GP may be able to prescribe exercise through one of the various 'exercise referral schemes' that are available. Some of the activities worth considering are swimming, cycling, walking, running, aerobics or yoga.

Summing it up

Many people find it helpful to summarise what they have learned about coping with panic attacks. As a final task, it's very useful to write up everything that you've learned so far. Think about any difficulties that you have already overcome; and any you expect to face in the future. Think about what you can do to manage these difficulties. Make notes so that you can refer back to them whenever you need to.

Remember, your self-help should not stop when you reach the end of this book – you'll need to continue facing up to feared situations and identifying and eliminating safety behaviours for as long as is necessary. It will be worth it.

Good luck!

Other Things that Might Help

This book has provided you with an introduction to the problems caused by panic attacks and what you can do to overcome them. Some people will find that this is all they need to do to see a big improvement while others may feel that they need a bit more information and help, and in that case there are some longer and more detailed self-help books around. Using self-help books, particularly those based on CBT, has been found to be particularly effective in the treatment of panic disorder. Ask your GP if there's a Books on Prescription scheme running in your area – if there isn't, we recommend the following books:

Panic Attacks: What They Are, Why They Happen And What You Can Do About Them by Christine Ingham, published by HarperCollins

Overcoming Panic by Derrick Silove and Vijaya Manicavasagar, published by Robinson

Coping Successfully with Panic Attacks (Overcoming Common Problems) by Shirley Trickett, published by Sheldon Press

Understanding Panic by David Westbrook and Khadija Rouf, published by Oxford Cognitive Therapy Centre (OCTC) (www.octc.co.uk/publications)

Sometimes the self help approach works better if you have someone supporting you. Ask your GP if there's anyone at the surgery who would be able to work through your self-help book with you.

Some surgeries have Graduate Mental Health Workers who would be able to help in this way, or who might offer general support. He or she is likely to be able to spend more time with you than your GP and may be able to offer follow-up appointments.

For some people a self-help approach may not be enough. If this is the case for you, don't despair – there are other kinds of help available.

Talk to your GP – make an appointment to talk through the different treatment options on offer to you. Your GP can refer you to an NHS therapist for Cognitive Behavioural Therapy – most places now have CBT available on the NHS, although there can be a considerable waiting list. Don't be put off if you've not found working through a

CBT-based self-help manual right for you – talking to a therapist can make a big difference. If an NHS therapist isn't available in your area or you'd prefer not to wait to see one, ask your GP to recommend a private therapist.

Although CBT is widely recommended for panic attacks, there are many other kinds of therapy available that you could also discuss with your GP.

Medication can be very helpful for some people and sometimes a combination of medication and psychological therapy can work wonders. However, you need to discuss this form of treatment and any possible side effects with your doctor to work out whether it's right for you.

The following organisations offer help and advice on panic disorder and you may find them a useful source of information:

Anxiety Care UK
Tel: 07552 877219
Email: admin@anxietycare.org.uk
Website: www.anxietycare.org.uk

British Association for Behavioural & Cognitive Psychotherapies (BABCP)
Provides contact details for therapists in your area, both NHS and private.
Tel: 0161 705 4304
Email: babcp@babcp.com
Website: www.babcp.com

Mind
Tel: 020 8519 2122
Website: www.mind.org.uk

An Introduction to Coping with Health Anxiety

2nd Edition

Brenda Hogan and Charles Young

ISBN: 978-1-47213-851-4 (paperback)
ISBN: 978-1-47213-952-8 (ebook)
Price: £4.99

This book offers guidance for those whose health anxiety or hypochondria have become serious problems and are having a negative impact on their mental health. Through the use of cognitive behavioural therapy (CBT), expert authors Brenda Hogan and Charles Young explain what health anxiety is and how it makes you feel, showing you how to spot and challenge thoughts that make you anxious and reduce your focus on illness. Written in a concise and accessible way, this book gives you both an understanding and an aid for combatting this often-neglected psychological problem.

An Introduction to Coping with Insomnia and Sleep Problems

2nd Edition

Colin Espie

ISBN: 978-1-47213-854-5 (paperback)

ISBN: 978-1-47213-892-7 (ebook)

Price: £4.99

Poor sleep can have a huge impact on our health and wellbeing, leaving us feeling run-down, exhausted and stressed out. Written by a leading expert in the field, this simple guide explains the causes of insomnia and why it is so difficult to break bad habits. It gives you clinically proven cognitive behavioural therapy (CBT) techniques for improving the quality of your sleep, showing you how to keep a sleep diary, set personal goals, improve your sleep hygiene, deal with a racing mind and make lasting improvements to your sleeping and waking pattern.

An Introduction to Coping with Phobias

2nd Edition

Brenda Hogan

ISBN: 978-1-47213-852-1 (paperback)

ISBN: 978-1-47213-881-1 (ebook)

Price: £4.99

It's very common for people to have a phobia of something – heights, spiders, water . . . but when that fear prevents you from doing the things you enjoy in life or causes you deep anxiety and feelings of panic, it's time to seek help. This book is a concise, authoritative guide for those whose phobia has become a debilitating problem, and shows you how cognitive behavioural therapy (CBT) can help you overcome your phobia. It encourages you to challenge the way you think and behave, including techniques on how to set your goals, face your fears, problem-solve and avoid relapses.